Hattie's Journey
The Courage to Keep Going

Dr. Felicia Williams-McGowan

Copyright © 2020 Dr. Felicia McGowan

All rights reserved. No part of this publication may be reproduced, distributed, or transmitted in any form or by any means, including photocopying, recording, or other electronic or mechanical methods, without the prior written permission of the publisher, except in the case of brief quotations embodied in critical reviews and certain other noncommercial uses permitted by copyright law.

ISBN-13: 978-1-63616-004-7

Published by Opportune Independent Publishing Company

For permission requests, write to the publisher, addressed "Attention: Permissions Coordinator" to the address below.

Email: Info@opportunepublishing.com

Address: 113 N. Live Oak Street
Houston, TX 77003

Dedication

I would like to thank the Almighty for giving me the strength to share this part of my journey. I dedicate this story to my deceased grandparents Guylen and Alice Williams. Also, to my grandmother Annie Mae (Bitum) Coley and deceased brother Reginald (Reggie) Van Williams. Bitum you always had the right words to say through your spirit. You kept me going when I wanted to give up.

Acknowledgments

I'd like to give a special acknowledgement to my Hattie's Ambassadors, Rev. Larry Robertson/Rev. Dwayne Brown, and members of Mt. Hebron Baptist Church in Rock Hill, SC for your continued support.

Thank you to everyone in Greenwood, SC who is so gracious with their support. Mr. & Mrs. Oscar Jones, Cardell (my husband), and Hattie (my mother) for being ready to pack my car continue to travel with Hattie's Journey.

What's Going On

"Come in and sit down Hattie, it's time for class to begin."

"Ok," Hattie stated as she walked into class passing Reggie, who was always working on puzzles. As Hattie begin to sit down she slumped over her desk. "Hey, Hattie what's wrong with you?" Nina asked.

"Nina, I'm in pain. Can you go get the school nurse to call my parents?"

Without asking the teacher, Nina ran down the hallway to get the school nurse for Hattie. Nurse Love quickly called 911 and Hattie's parents. Soon, the ambulance arrived at school and Hattie was taken to the local hospital.

Once she was there, Dr. Left explained to Hattie and her parents that her blood work was different. He did not understand what was going on and suggested to Hattie's parents that she be flown to Destunee Medical Center.

Without thinking about it, Hattie's parents agreed that was the best thing to do. She was flown to Destunee Medical Center to see Dr. Biggs. When Hattie arrived at the hospital Dr. Biggs took her temperature and had blood drawn to try and understand what was going on with Hattie. After waiting for hours, Dr. Biggs told Hattie and her parents that her kidney she received from her mother was losing its function and that she had to go back on dialysis again. Hattie asked the doctor, "What do you mean dialysis again?"

As Hattie listened to the doctor, tears rolled down her face as she did not want to lose the gift that her mother had given her. She thought to herself, life is too good right now to go on dialysis again. She began to think about the process of having the surgery to get the tube in her stomach again and switching out the bags 5 times a day. She was not happy! Especially with Summer break being a couple of weeks away.

When Hattie was released from the hospital, Hattie's mother visited her teacher. Hattie's mother picked up summer reading and explained to Ms. Hope that Hattie is in for a long summer but, she will get through it.

Summer

Hattie thought about the first time she had to go through this and how she kept it together. But like any other journey, sometimes it is hard to understand why problems get in the way. Like most teenagers, Hattie was going through her own issues and dialysis was far from her mind.

Hattie didn't want to discuss her medical concerns with anyone. She did not want any of her friends to feel sorry for her, especially Nina. Hattie's mother suggested that she go to visit her grandmother in Georgia to get her mind off of things. Hattie's mother told her to remember that everything happens for a reason.

When Hattie arrived back home and began to wrap her mind around what was going on, she decided to finally called Nina. Nina was very upset with Hattie because they had been best friends since kindergarten and ignoring her phone calls was unacceptable.

"Hattie, what is going on with you? Reggie, Dell, and I have been so worried," said Nina. "What is going on with your health?"

"It's my kidney" Hattie explained. "It's losing its function and the doctor has placed me back on dialysis."

Hattie told Nina that being on dialysis is a constant reminder of how she could not be a normal kid. Like most teenagers, Hattie wanted to hang out at the mall, go skating, and be with friends. Nina reminded Hattie how she overcame this before and told her that she can do it again.

Hattie's parents took her to a doctor's appointment before leaving for her trip. Instead of Dr. Biggs discussing kidney function, he wanted to focus on Hattie's emotional and social wellbeing. Since Hattie had known Dr. Biggs since she was twelve he was like a father to her. Hattie always took Dr. Biggs seriously, especially when he looked at her square in the eyes and discussed her health.

Dr. Biggs explained to Hattie, "I have been knowing you for a long time and you are too strong to let this disease beat you."

Grandma's House

While riding to Georgia, Hattie thought about the conversation she had with Dr. Biggs and started to feel sorry for herself. She knew she could not let that happen.

As she finally arrived at Bitum's (this is what all the grandkids called their grandmother), she walked towards her grandma and said, "I am so upset and don't want to do dialysis, it's too much!"

Bitum was a strong woman. She hugged Hattie and said, "Everything is going to be fine don't you worry about that."

Hattie smiled at her grandmother and said, "I hope to be strong like you one day."

Bitum explained to Hattie that she is a survivor and this is just another setback in her journey for her to overcome. Bitum told Hattie, "Your kidney is just taking a small break baby there is no need to worry about it. You will be fine."

Hattie thanked Bitum for her comfort and she knew that she would get through it she just didn't know how. On Hattie's last day of her visit at Bitum's house, they sat on the front porch waiting on her mother to come pick her up. The warm wind blew across their faces on that summer day. "What a wonderful day," said Bitum.

"It would be even better if I could just hang out with my friends and not worry about my illness," said Hattie.

"Baby everything happens for a reason," Bitum told Hattie, "Your kidney is just taking a break. Just wait and see!"

Remember to keep the faith as you go through your journey.

Hattie felt that the trip was good for her. On the way home, she thought about her conversation with Bitum that everything was going to be alright. Hattie loved her grandmother and she was happy that she was able to spend time with her.

Nina's House

When Hattie arrived home the first person she called was Nina. She wanted to catch up with what she had missed while she was in Georgia for the summer.

Instead of Nina answering the question, she changed the subject and asked Hattie, "How is the dialysis, and how have you been feeling?" Hattie told Nina what Bitum had said and how their talk has given her the courage to keep going.

Nina asked Hattie to come over to her house to hang out. Since they lived in the same neighborhood, Hattie put on her favorite tennis shoes and begin to walk to Nina's home.

When Hattie arrived at Nina's house, Reggie and Dell were outside. They all went inside and hung out in her bright pink room. While the boys were texting friends, Nina and Hattie looked at outfits. They were having fun and Hattie loved seeing her friends that she missed all summer. Nina, Reggie and Dell were happy that they could take Hattie's mind off of her health concerns even though it was only for a short period of time.

Doctor's Visit

Two weeks before school started, Hattie traveled to her monthly check-up with her mother. When she arrived Dr. Biggs wanted to check to make sure that dialysis was working properly. He spoke with Hattie about how she was feeling Hattie explained to the doctor that she had been going to the bathroom more.

The doctor looked confused but, told Hattie he would he would check her kidney to see what was going on.

Hattie thanked Dr. Biggs for listening but, she felt he didn't believe her. When Hattie and her mother traveled back home she had a big smile on her face. Hattie began to think about what Bitum had told her about her kidney taking a break.

Hattie's mother knew that she was a special child and that her life was different. Mrs. Osborn did not want her daughter to be disappointed with the news from the doctor.

Hattie was hopeful that her kidney was working again. She knew in her heart that her kidney was back on track and she continued to get excited as she thought of the getting off of dialysis. While Hattie and her mother were talking they were interrupted by the phone ringing. It was the doctor's office.

The Results

The results indicated that Hattie's kidney function was back to normal. Hattie was taken off of dialysis before school started. Hattie was excited and cried with tears of joy. Dr. Biggs told them that this was short of amazing and he had never known anything like this to happen to any of his other patients. Hattie explained to Dr. Biggs that her grandmother told her that her kidney was taking a break.

Dr. Biggs laughed and said, "Maybe it did."

On the way home, Hattie called her grandmother to share the good news. Bitum told Hattie, baby remember to never give up and continue to travel through your journey. Hattie was thrilled to know that she could look forward to going back to school, being with her friends, and not be on dialysis.

Hattie met Nina, Reggie, and Dell at the mall and shared the good news with them too. Her friends hugged her and told her that they knew things would work out. As the crew walked through the mall in anticipation of the new school year, they were excited to see Hattie back being happy again.

New Year

Hattie got up bright and early on the first day of school. The sun peeped through her window and light bounced off of her brown eyes. Hattie was like any other teenager on the first day of school. She had the perfect outfit that matched her teal blue head band. Hattie pulled her hair back with a puff at the top. Which was her favorite hairstyle.

Hattie went to the kitchen and sat down to eat her grits that her mother cooked every morning. Then Hattie took her medicine which she dared not to miss after understanding how easy it is for her kidney to stop working. Hattie hugged and kissed her mother and told her goodbye. Hattie drove to Nina's house to pick her up for school.

When Hattie and Nina arrived at school, Reggie and Dell were standing on the side of the building waiting for them. When the morning bell ranged they all walked to their classes. Hattie stood in the doorway and thought about her busy summer. Her teacher Ms. Faith interrupted her and said, "Come in Hattie and sit down, its time for class to begin."

"Okay." Hattie stated as she sat down in class to listen to the morning announcements.

THE END

Hattie's Journey: The Courage to Keep Going
By Dr. Felicia Williams McGowan

This story can be used individually or with the activity book to help open the dialogue about kidney health and the importance of friends and family.

Questions for Discussion
1. Why do you think Hattie was unhappy at the beginning of the story?
2. Who did Hattie visit during the summer?
3. Who were Hattie's best friends? What did Hattie and her friends do together?
4. Who are your friends and what do you and your friends do together?

Definitions

Dialysis is the process of filtering wastes and extra fluid from the body by means other than the kidneys. Sometimes, a **transplanted kidney** may stop working, and the child may need to return to dialysis. Transplantation may be delayed if a matching kidney is not available or if the child has an infectious disease or an active **kidney disease** that has progressed rapidly.

Peritoneal dialysis uses the lining of the abdominal cavity—the space in the body that holds organs such as the stomach, intestines, and liver—to filter the blood. The lining is called the peritoneum. A kind of salty water called dialysis solution is emptied from a plastic bag through a catheter—a thin, flexible tube—into the abdominal cavity. While it is inside, the **dialysis** solution soaks up wastes and extra fluid from the body. After a few hours, the used **dialysis** solution is drained into another bag, removing the wastes and extra fluid from the body. The abdomen is filled with fluid all day and all night, so the filtering process never stops. The process of draining and refilling, called an exchange, takes about 30 minutes.

National Institute of Diabetes and Digestive and Kidney Disease (March 12, 2014). *Treatment Of Methods of Kidney Transplants in Children.* http://www.niddk.nih.gov/health-information/health-topics/kidneydisease/ treatment-methods-for-kidney-failure-in-children/Pages/facts.aspx#2

Hattie's Journey: The Courage to Keep Going
By Dr. Felicia Williams McGowan

Dr. McGowan is a 9x published author of Hattie's Journey Stories/Coloring/Activity and journal books. The stories are created around a little girl who loved school and all things fun and spending time with her amazing friends. Experiencing a roadblock in her journey caused Hattie to reroute her path and learn how to handle things differently early in her life. Hattie's Journey books can be used to familiarize readers of the different ups and downs families could face when a child has been diagnosed with kidney failure or any other disease that will disrupt the child and their families lives. Dr. McGowan inspires others through mentorships, workshops, and her stories of faith as she travels through her own journey.

Drwilliamsmcgowan@gmail.com
www.drfeliciawilliamsmcgowan.com